ABIGAIL ADAMS

Adviser to a President

Colonial Profiles Series

Dennis Brindell Fradin

Illustrations by Tom Dunnington
Picture Research: Judith B. Fradin

ENSLOW PUBLISHERS, INC.

Bloy St. & Ramsey Ave.
Box 777
Hillside, N.J. 07205
U.S.A.

P.O. Box 38
Aldershot
Hants GU12 6BP
U.K.

Library of Congress Cataloging-in-Publication Data

Fradin, Dennis B.

Abigail Adams: adviser to a president / by Dennis Brindell Fradin.

p. cm. — (Colonial profiles)

Includes index.

Summary: Examines the life and achievements of the wife of the second American president.

ISBN 0-89490-228-8

1. Adams, Abigail, 1744-1818—Juvenile literature. 2. Presidents—United States—Wives—Biography—Juvenile literature. 3. Adams, John, 1735-1826—Juvenile literature. (1. Adams, Abigail, 1744-1818. 2. First ladies.) I. Title II. Series: Fradin, Dennis B. Colonial profiles.

E322.1.A38F73 1989

973.4'4'0924—dc19

(B) 88-31331

CIP

AC

Printed in the United States of America

10 9 8 7 6 5 4 3 2 1

Illustration Credits:

Tom Dunnington (illustrator), pp. 8, 15, 23, 26, 33, 42; Historical Pictures Service, Chicago, pp. 13, 19; Library of Congress, pp. 9, 12, 17, 22, 25, 29, 34, 38, 40; Massachusetts Historical Society, pp. 4, 14, 24; The National Portrait Gallery, Smithsonian Institution, p. 44; U.S. Department of the Interior, National Park Service, Adams National Historic Site, Quincy, Massachusetts, pp. 31, 35, 39.

Cover Illustration by Tom Dunnington.

Contents

Abigail Adams at age 22

Introduction

In colonial America, girls and women lacked the rights they have today. Women could not vote. They could not serve as lawmakers. Most girls received little or no schooling. Females could not go to college.

A few girls had good educations anyway. Most of them were taught at home. Abigail Smith of Massachusetts was taught at home by her parents. She became one of the best-read women in the 13 colonies.

When nearly 20, Abigail married John Adams. Soon after, America began to break free of England. John Adams played a key role in the birth of the United States. He had to spend long periods away from home to do this. Abigail and John Adams wrote letters to each other when apart.

Thanks to their letters, we know much about Abigail and John. We know that Abigail was one of the first Americans to speak out for women's rights. She also spoke out for the rights of black people. Women and blacks had to fight for many years for the rights Abigail thought they deserved.

In 1796 John Adams was elected president of the United States. Abigail then became the country's First Lady. She and John were the first to live in the White House in Washington, D.C. They were also the parents of John Quincy Adams, the nation's sixth president. Abigail Adams remains the only woman who was wife to one president and mother to another.

A Love for Books

Abigail Smith was born in 1744 in Weymouth, Massachusetts. She had an older sister and a younger sister. She also had a younger brother. Her father was a minister and her mother a homemaker.

There were schools near Abigail's home. Other girls learned some reading and writing at these schools. Abigail's parents kept her out of school. For one thing, she was sick a lot. They thought she would get sick more often if she mixed with children at school. Also, town schools were not very good in those days, so they wanted to teach her themselves.

Soon after Abigail learned to talk, her mother taught her the alphabet. Abigail was very bright. She quickly went from reading simple words to simple books to harder books.

Abigail's father had a large library. Abigail loved to sit in his library with him while he

Abigail reading with her mother

worked. As Reverend Smith wrote his sermons, Abigail read his books. He often took time to talk about the books with Abigail. She became one of the best-read young ladies in the 13 colonies.

Since her parents did not let Abigail play with

Boston in the time of Abigail Adams

other children, she was often with older relatives. On Sundays, Abigail listened to her father's sermons in church. During the week, the minister's wife had the job of visiting sick and poor people. Abigail went with her mother on these visits. They helped her develop strong feelings for unfortunate people.

Abigail also spent time with her aunt and uncle in Boston, the Massachusetts capital. The visits she liked best were to Grandmother and Grandfather Quincy in the town of Braintree, Massachusetts. Abigail felt that Grandmother Quincy was one of the few people who understood her.

Abigail's parents were upset with her much of the time. Abigail was moody. She was stubborn. She was often angry at them. Abigail felt she had cause to be upset. She wanted to play with other children. She thought her parents worried too much about her health.

Grandmother Quincy agreed that Abigail was moody and stubborn, but she was happy about it! She was glad that Abigail had a mind of her own.

Abigail Meets John Adams

Once Abigail reached her teens, her parents let her make friends outside her family. She made some friends while visiting her aunt and uncle in Boston. Abigail and her friends had something in common. They loved books and wanted to improve their minds.

There were no telephones back then. But Abigail and her friends found a way to share their thoughts when apart. They wrote letters to each other. They wrote about the young men they liked. They told their secret thoughts. They did not sign their real names to these letters. Each girl chose a "pen name." Abigail's was Diana—after the Roman goddess of the moon.

When Abigail was 15, she met a young man at a party. His name was John Adams. John had grown up in Braintree, where her grandparents lived. He was 24 years old and had just become a lawyer.

At first Abigail and John did not like each

John Adams, later the second president of the United States

other much. John preferred Abigail's cousin, Hannah Quincy. John annoyed Abigail by acting much older and wiser than she. But when Abigail was 17, the two came to like each other very, very much.

Abigail and John were a lot alike. They both loved books. They both had strong opinions. They both liked to express their thoughts to others. John became a regular visitor to the Smith house. He often brought Abigail books. The next time he came, they would talk about the books.

Soon Abigail and John were not just talking

Abigail Adams was intelligent and beautiful.

about books. They walked through meadows and talked about themselves. They sat under trees and kissed. When they were apart, they wrote love letters.

A sweet love letter that John wrote on October 4, 1762, still exists. He called her "Miss Adorable" in this letter. He also complained to

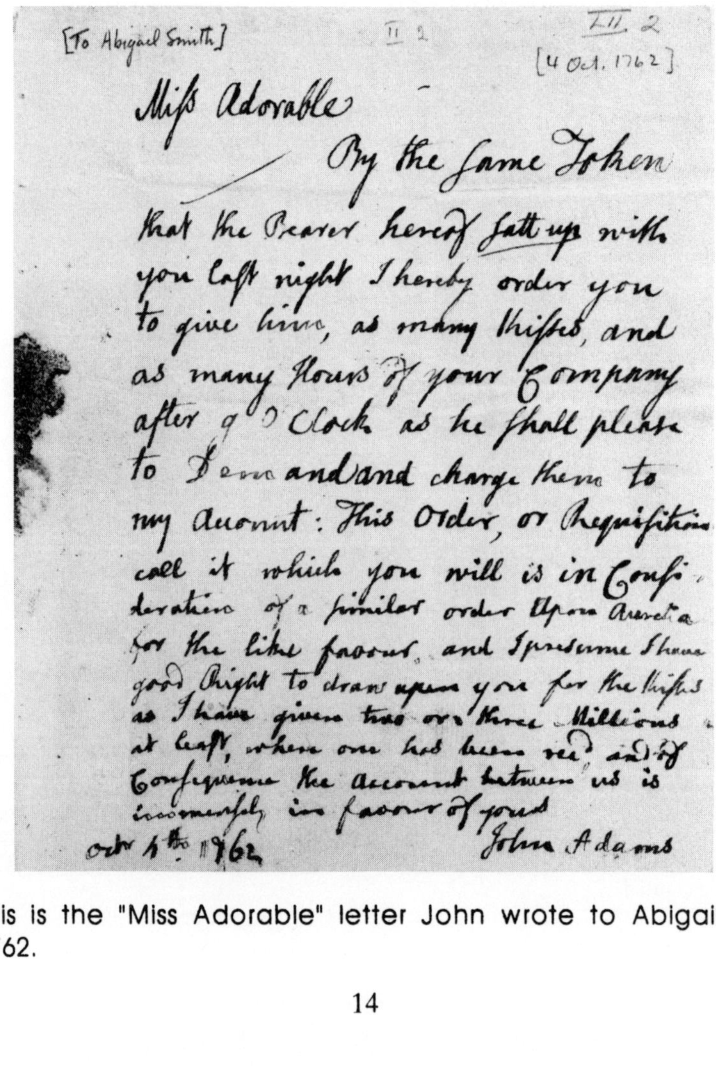

[To Abigail Smith]

[4 Oct. 1762]

Miss Adorable

By the same Token that the Bearer hereof satt up with you last night I hereby order you to give him, as many Kisses, and as many Hours of your Company after 9 O Clock as he shall please to Demand and charge them to my Account: This Order, or Requisition call it which you will is in Consideration of a similar order Upon Aurelia for the like favour, and I presume I have good Right to draw upon you for the Kisses as I have given two or three Millions at least, when one has been received, and of Consequence the Account between us is immensely in favour of yours

John Adams

Octr 4th. 1762

This is the "Miss Adorable" letter John wrote to Abigail in 1762.

Abigail and John fell in love.

Abigail. He said she gave him only one kiss for every "two or three million" he gave her!

By this time, they were planning to marry. They put it off for a while, though. John wanted to earn a better living before marrying. Abigail's parents thought she was too young to marry. They may have thought that John was not good enough for her.

The wedding took place when Abigail was almost 20. Abigail's father married them. Now she was no longer Abigail Smith. She had the name by which she is known to history—Abigail Adams.

Children and Politics

The newlyweds moved to Braintree—John's hometown. They lived on the farm where John had grown up. The farm provided their milk, eggs, and vegetables. They did not support themselves by farming. John's work as a lawyer was the way the family earned money.

The farm where newlyweds John and Abigail Adams lived

Abigail liked being married. She and John still went on walks. Sometimes, they sat on Penn's Hill near their home and looked at Boston, about 10 miles away. In the winter, they sledded. Abigail and John also began to produce a family very soon.

Their first child was born nine months after the wedding. They named her Abigail. Since having two Abigails in a family was confusing, they called her Nabby. Later Abigail and John had four more children. Three were sons—John Quincy, Charles, and Thomas Boylston Adams. They also had another daughter, Susanna, who lived just a year.

One thing that upset Abigail was that John was often away from home. She knew he could not help it, though. He rode from town to town working as a lawyer. He also went to many political meetings in Boston.

John and Abigail had married in troubled times. England—the country that ruled the colonies—needed money. To raise it, England taxed the Americans. From 1764 to 1773 England passed many tax laws. Americans were to pay taxes on such items as sugar, tea, and even newspapers.

Along with other Americans, John and Abigail hated these taxes. John entered politics so that he

Americans who were angry about British rule raised "liberty poles" and then gathered around them for patriotic speeches.

could fight for America's rights. In 1770 he was elected to be a Massachusetts lawmaker. He was soon one of the colony's best-known lawmakers.

By 1774 it looked as though there might be a war with England. Americans planned a big meeting to talk things over. Every colony was asked to send delegates to this meeting. John Adams was one of the four from Massachusetts.

This meeting was called the First Continental Congress. It opened in September 1774 in Philadelphia, Pennsylvania. Abigail and John were apart for several months while he attended it. They exchanged letters during that time. Abigail told John about the news from Massachusetts. He told her about events in Congress and asked her advice on congressional matters.

The First Continental Congress met until late October 1774. John Adams and the other men then went home. They planned to meet again in the spring if England did not change its ways.

The Birth of a New Country

England would not give in. War with England began on April 19, 1775. The first battle took place at Lexington, Massachusetts. America fought this war—the Revolutionary War—to free itself from England.

Soon after the Battle of Lexington, John and Abigail parted again. John went to Philadelphia to the Second Continental Congress. He played a key role at this meeting. He helped form the American army. He also helped Thomas Jefferson of Virginia create the Declaration of Independence. This paper said that the 13 colonies were now the United States.

Abigail was very busy while John was in Congress. She ran the farm. She did all the child raising. Abigail taught the children to read, using such books as *Giles Gingerbread.* Once they knew how, she had them read aloud to her every day. Abigail also made sure that the children, in-

The Americans (in the front) lost the Battle of Lexington to the British (firing their guns).

cluding Nabby, learned Latin. It was rare for a girl to know Latin back then.

As time passed, Abigail became bolder in her letters to John. She began to tell him what she thought the congressmen should do. John loved Abigail's spirit, but he sometimes thought she was too outspoken for a woman. Today, though, many

Abigail reading to Nabby and little John Qunicy Adams

of Abigail's views seem on target. In fact, she was way ahead of her time in some ways.

Abigail wrote her most famous letter to John on March 31, 1776. She had two things to say about the new country Congress was creating. She said that slavery was wrong. She said that women should have more rights. "Remember the Ladies," she wrote. She even hinted that women should be allowed to vote.

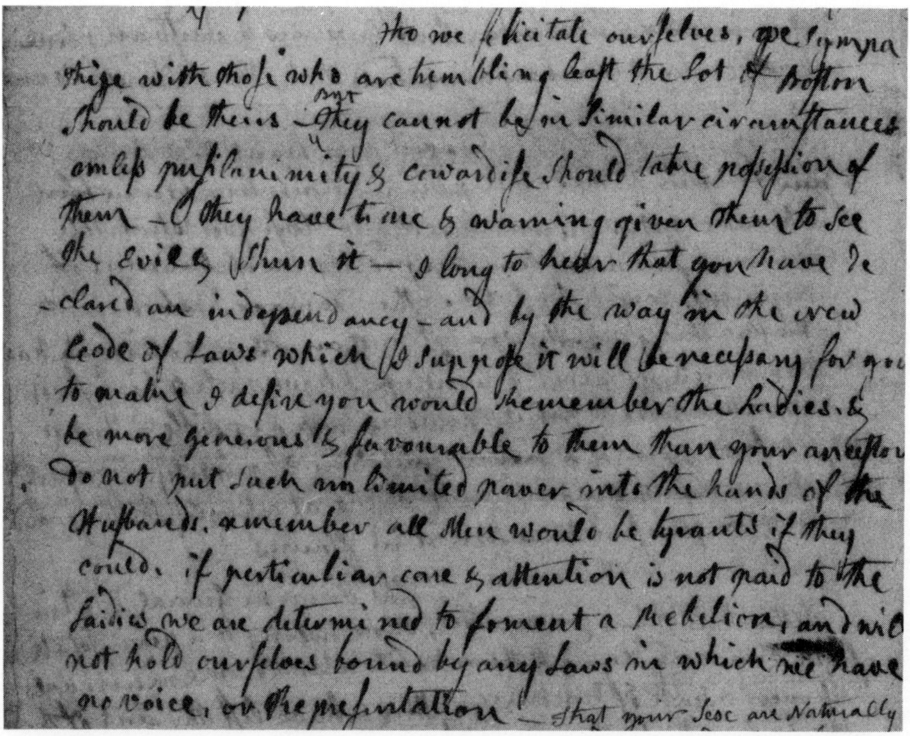

tho we felicitate ourselves, we sympa
thize with those who are trembling least the Lot of Boston
should be theirs—but they cannot be in similar circumstances
unless pusilanimity & cowardise should take possession of
them—they have time & warning given them to see
the Evil & shun it—I long to hear that you have de
-clared an independancy—and by the way in the new
Code of Laws which I suppose it will be necessary for you
to make I desire you would Remember the Ladies, &
be more generous & favourable to them than your ancestors
Do not put such unlimited power into the hands of the
Husbands. remember all Men would be tyrants if they
could. if perticuliar care & attention is not paid to the
Laidies we are determined to foment a Rebelion, and will
not hold ourselves bound by any Laws in which we have
no voice, or Representation—That your Sex are Naturally

This is Abigail's famous "Remember the Ladies" letter. To see the handwritten words "Remember the Ladies," look at the end of the 9th line from the top (8th line from the bottom).

Congress as a whole was not as fair as Abigail. John Adams and many other northerners hated slavery. Many southerners wanted to keep it. The result was that Congress would not ban slavery. As for more rights for women, few congressmen favored that. Women and black people had to wait many years before winning their rights.

A slave being sold. Abigail spoke out against slavery.

John Quincy Adams marching with the soldiers on the family farm

Abigail also did her part to help fight the war. She let soldiers stay in her home. One night she housed a whole company. The next day Abigail watched as her eight-year-old son, John Quincy, marched with the soldiers near the house. For a while, though, it appeared that America would go back to being 13 colonies. The country was losing the war.

Later, things improved for the Americans. France, which hated England, began to think about helping the Americans. With France's help, the Americans could win.

In late 1777, Congress let John go home for a while. He returned to the Braintree farm. The congressmen were not paid, so his family needed money. John hoped to do some law work before returning to Congress. However, a letter from Congress soon arrived. Congress wanted John to cross the ocean and get France on America's side.

The Trips to Europe

Abigail and John talked it over. Winter voyages were dangerous. Besides, the English might try to capture John. But since it might help the country, they decided that John must go. They also decided that John Quincy would go along to help his father in France.

Kitchen of Abigail and John Adams

In February 1778 Abigail said good-bye to John and her 10-year-old son. John and John Quincy Adams boarded the *Boston.* The ship set sail for France, 3,000 miles away.

During the next months Abigail heard only bad news. People said John had been killed. In fact, that had almost happened. At sea, the *Boston* got into a fight with a British ship. John took out his musket and went out on deck with John Quincy. Suddenly, a cannonball flew by. Had it been a few feet closer, it might have killed two future United States presidents.

It turned out that this trip was not needed! When he arrived in France, John learned that Ben Franklin of Pennsylvania had already obtained French aid. John and his son sailed home in summer 1779. They returned to their family in August.

A few weeks later, John was asked to return to Europe. By then, it looked as though America might win. John was to make peace with England. The Americans hoped that England would end the war and admit that the United States was a new country.

Again Abigail and John talked. They decided that John Quincy should again go along. He knew French and could help his father. John

Quincy did not want to go back to Europe, though. He wanted to enter Harvard College.

Abigail was a very loving mother. She was also one who had strong ideas about what was right and wrong. She told John Quincy that it was his duty to go. She said his father and his country needed him. Twelve-year-old John Quincy listened. By the time his mother was done, he felt like a criminal for arguing! Abigail and John decided that nine-year-old Charles should go, too.

John and the two boys sailed in November 1779. Again, they almost did not make it. This time their ship leaked. But they reached Europe,

John Quincy Adams, the son of Abigail and John, as a young man. Later John Quincy Adams became the sixth president of the United States.

where they had many adventures. Among other things, John helped make a peace treaty with England. This treaty was approved in 1783. It meant that the United States had won its war for independence.

Charles had become homesick and had sailed home by then. John and John Quincy stayed in Europe. John Adams had to make deals with European nations.

Abigail and John remained apart for several years. This was their longest time apart. Abigail ran the farm and raised the children while John worked in Europe. At times her money ran low. She had John send her lace and cloth from Europe. She sold these goods around Braintree. The money helped pay the family's bills.

Abigail knew that John had to stay in Europe as long as Congress wanted. She grew very lonely. Finally, she could no longer bear to be away from John. In early 1784 Abigail decided to cross the ocean with Nabby. The other two boys would stay in Massachusetts with relatives.

Mother and daughter sailed in June 1784. They reached England a month later. Imagine how thrilled Abigail was when she and Nabby met John and John Quincy in London. She had not seen her husband and oldest son for nearly five years!

The happy family reunion in England

The Adamses spent about three years in Europe. They lived a few months near Paris, where John had more work to do. Most of the time they lived in London, where John served as U.S. minister to England.

Abigail compared every place she saw in Europe to the United States. She loved her country so much that she thought no place was nearly as good. The theaters and operas of Paris were enjoyable. But she thought Paris was too dirty.

As for England, Abigail was slow to forgive that country for the Revolutionary War. Not only

George III, king of England

Nabby as a young woman

that, she thought many of the English looked down on Americans. She hated having to wait four hours just to meet the king and queen.

Abigail was also upset when Nabby got married in England. Nabby married an American. She moved just a few blocks away. But like her own mother, Abigail had a hard time letting her children leave home.

Abigail cheered up when Nabby had a baby in England. She loved helping to care for her grandson. Abigail grew happier still when the family left England in spring 1788. She was eager to return to her favorite place in the world. Of course, that was Massachusetts in the United States.

First Lady of the United States

John came home a hero. Cannons were fired as their ship entered Boston. Thousands of people came to greet John and Abigail. They loved John for doing so much for the new country.

In 1789 John was elected the first vice-president of the United States. He served under George Washington, the first president. John and Abigail were not happy about his new job. They thought the country gave the vice-president too little work. Besides, the job did not pay much. During John's first four years as vice-president, he and Abigail went into debt.

One problem was that the vice-president had to rent the house where he and his family stayed. Abigail and John could not afford this. During John's second term, he rented rooms in Philadelphia, which was then the U.S. capital. Abigail ran the family farm. John spent time with his family in Massachusetts whenever he could.

Living this way, John and Abigail even saved a little money.

In 1796, an election was held to choose the second president. John Adams barely beat Thomas Jefferson. This meant that Adams would be president and Jefferson would be vice-president.

Near the time of the vote count, Abigail had a battle of her own. She had taught a black servant named James to read and write. She enrolled James in a school, but some neighbors complained. They did not want their children in school with a black person.

President John Adams

Abigail was enraged. She yelled at a neighbor who asked her to take James out of the school. Black as well as white people could go to heaven, she said. So why shouldn't schools admit black people? She convinced her neighbors that James should go to the school.

In spring 1797 John and Abigail moved into the presidential mansion in Philadelphia. Abigail was now the country's First Lady. She and John thought that the First Family should not act as though they were better than other people. They had to give parties at the presidential mansion, but they kept them simple. Visitors were more likely

Abigail Adams when John was president

The White House as it looked a few years after John and Abigail Adams lived in it

to have a good talk with President and Mrs. Adams than a fancy meal.

Near the end of John's presidency, Washington, D.C., became the nation's capital. John and Abigail moved into a big house in the new capital. They were the first to live in this White House. Abigail loved the White House and said it was built "for ages to come." She was right. The White House is still home to the U.S. president and his family.

Joy and Sadness in Her Last Years

In spring of 1801 Abigail and John returned home. Their part of Braintree had been renamed Quincy, for Abigail's Grandfather Quincy. Abigail and John spent the rest of their lives quietly in a house called Peacefield.

Abigail was no longer the United States' First Lady. She was still "First Lady" of the Adams family, though! Even after her children married, she told them where to live (near her). She told them how to live. She even planned her grandchildren's lives. Abigail usually got her way. But her meddling sometimes caused trouble. For example, Abigail and John Quincy planned how John Quincy's children should be educated. The problem was that they did not tell John Quincy's wife about it!

Abigail was as loving as she was bossy, though. She was usually forgiven for telling her family how to live their lives.

Abigail had some sadness in her later years. Her son Charles had died in 1800 at just 30 years of age. In 1811 Nabby became ill with cancer. Nabby died in 1813 at the age of just 48.

Abigail and John helped raise several of their grandchildren. Other grandchildren lived with them from time to time. "Grandmama" Abigail sat and read with her grandchildren. She bragged about them when they learned their letters or did something else special.

Her grandchildren could do no wrong in Abigail's eyes. Abigail wrote that she was happy

An elderly Abigail Adams reading to her grandchildren

that one of John Quincy's children was "a wild Boy." As Grandmother Quincy had felt about her, Abigail was glad that he had a mind of his own. She wrote that a boy who acted too good might turn out to be a "dull old man."

Abigail lived to see her son, John Quincy Adams, become one of the nation's top lawmakers. She saw him serve in the U.S. Senate and as secretary of state. John Adams lived to see John Quincy elected the sixth U.S. president in 1825. But Abigail did not get to see that. Surrounded by her family, she died on October 28, 1818. She was almost 74 years old. She and John had been married for 54 years and three days.

Abigail had asked John to one day burn her letters. Luckily, he did not do it. Thanks largely to her letters, Abigail is now hailed as an early American fighter for human rights.

Many of the letters Abigail and John sent each other can be read in books. Abigail seems to come alive for people who read her letters. You can hear Abigail telling John to "Remember the Ladies." You can hear her arguing for the rights of black people. And you can picture her giving John a kiss for every "two or three million" he gave her.

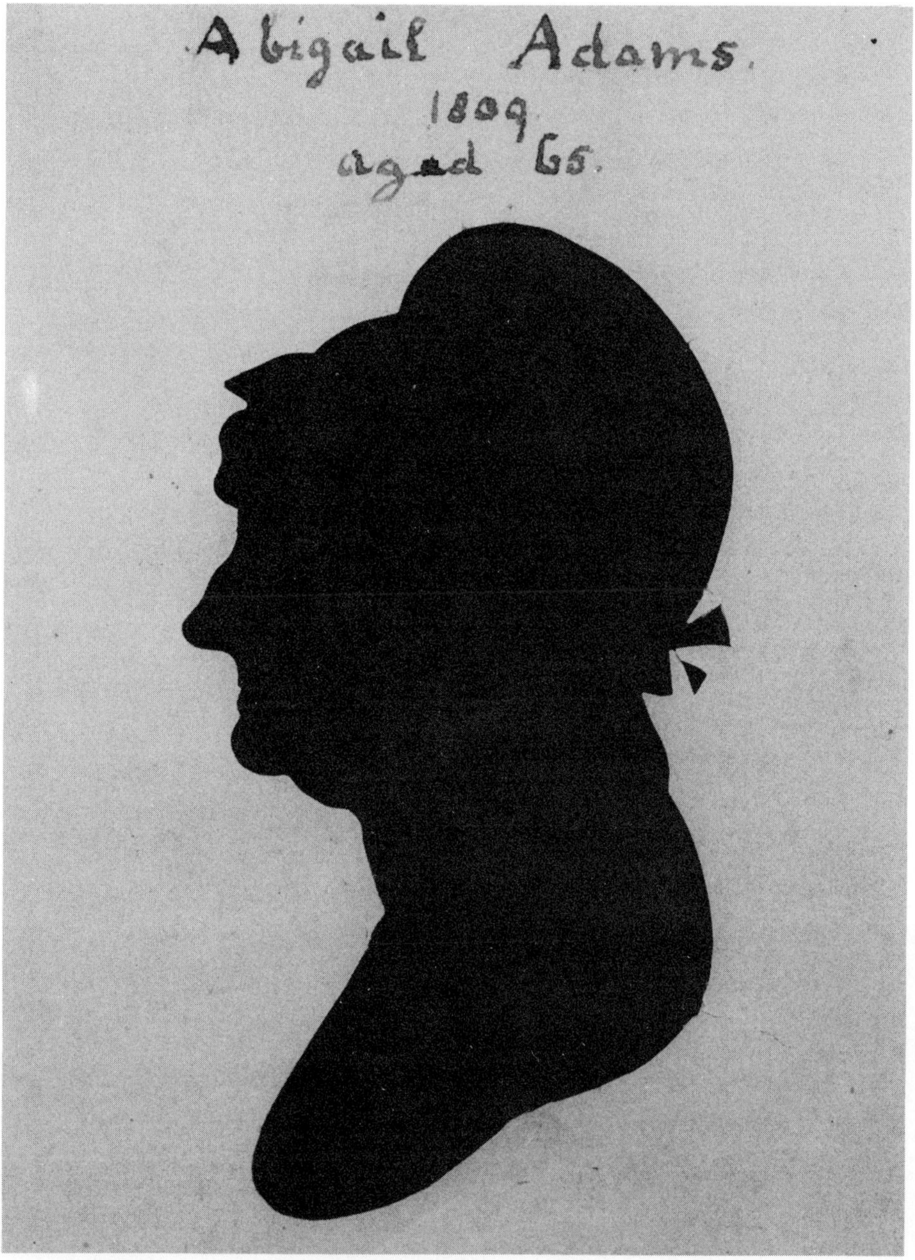

Abigail Adams' silhouette, made in 1809 when she was 65 years old

Important Dates

1744 Abigail is born in Weymouth, Massachusetts.

1764 Abigail marries John Adams.

1765 Abigail and John's first child, Nabby, is born; later will come John Quincy, Susanna (who doesn't live long), Charles, and Thomas Boylston Adams.

1774 John is chosen to be a Massachusetts delegate to the Continental Congress.

1775 Revolutionary War starts.

1776 Abigail writes her famous "Remember the Ladies" letter; this year John helps Thomas Jefferson create the Declaration of Independence.

1781 The United States wins the Revolutionary War.

1784 Abigail and Nabby join John and John Quincy Adams in London.

1788 Abigail and John return to America.

1789 John Adams is elected first U.S. vice-president.

1796 John Adams is elected second U.S. president; Abigail becomes the First Lady.

1800 Abigail's son Charles dies.

1801 Abigail and John return home to Quincy (formerly Braintree), Massachusetts.

1813 Nabby dies.

1818 Abigail dies, at the age of almost 74.

1825 Abigail's son John Quincy Adams is elected sixth U.S. president.

Glossary

adorable—lovable and wonderful.

capital—the city where laws are made for a country, state, or colony.

colonies—settlements built by a country outside its borders.

Continental Congress—the lawmaking body which first met in 1774 and ran the country before the U.S. Congress was created.

Declaration of Independence—the paper that said the 13 colonies had become the United States of America.

delegates—people who are sent to act for others.

First Lady—a nickname for the U.S. president's wife.

independence—freedom.

minister—The term *minister* can refer to a religious leader. It can also refer to someone who represents a country in a foreign land.

musket—an old-fashioned type of rifle that was used during the Revolutionary War.

politics—the science of winning and holding public offices.

Revolutionary War—the war the 13 colonies fought against England to become the United States of America.

13 colonies—England's colonies in America before the Revolutionary War.

voyage—in Abigail's day, this meant a trip by ship.

INDEX